HOW TO IMPROVE AT GOLF

All the information you need to know to get on top of your game!

More than just instructional guides, the **HOW TO IMPROVE AT...** series gives you everything you need to achieve your goals—tips on technique, step-by-step demonstrations, nutritional advice, and the secrets of successful pro athletes. Excellent visual instructions and expert advice combine to act as your own personal trainer. These books aim to give you the know-how and confidence to improve your performance.

Studies have shown that an active approach to life makes you feel happier and less stressed. The easiest way to start is by taking up a new sport or improving your skills in an existing one. You simply have to choose an activity that enthuses you.

HOW TO IMPROVE AT GOLF does not promise instant success. It simply gives you the tools to become the best at whatever you choose to do.

Every care has been taken to ensure that these instructions are safe to follow, but in the event of injury Crabtree Publishing shall not be liable for any injuries or damages.

By Peter Parks

Crabtree Publishing Company

www.crabtreebooks.com

Cover: Golf star Tiger Woods
Special thank you to: Hever Castle Golf Club, Kent
Anna Brett, Sophie Furse, Joe Harris, Hayley Terry, John
Lingham, Elizabeth Knowles and Gareth Randall
Photography: Sarah Williams
Illustrations: Nick Owen
Photo credits: Actionplus: front cover; Andy Altenburger/
Icon SMI/ Corbis: p. 13 bottom; Rick Barrentine/ Corbis: p. 40 top; Brent Foster/ Reuters/ Corbis: p. 45 center right; iStock: p. 41 top, p. 45 bottom; Ellen Ozler/ Reuters/ Corbis: p. 42 top; Rex Features: p. 43 bottom; Tony Roberts/ Corbis: p. 43 center; Shutterstock: p. 7 center right, p. 8 center left, p. 9 center right, p. 39 top, p. 39 center, p. 2, p. 39 bottom right, p. 40 bottom left, p. 40 bottom right, p. 43 top. Chris Trotman/ Newsport/ Corbis: p. 42 bottom; Larry Williams/ Corbis: p. 45 top.

Library and Archives Canada Cataloguing in Publication

Parks, Peter
   How to improve at golf / Peter Parks.

(How to improve at--)
Includes index.
ISBN 978-0-7787-3567-0 (bound).--ISBN 978-0-7787-3589-2 (pbk.)

   1. Golf--Training--Juvenile literature. I. Title. II. Series.

GV968.P37 2007   j796.352   C2007-906482-5

Library of Congress Cataloging-in-Publication Data

Parks, Peter.
   How to improve at golf / Peter Parks.
      p. cm. -- (How to improve at--)
   Includes index.
   ISBN-13: 978-0-7787-3567-0 (rlb)
   ISBN-10: 0-7787-3567-2 (rlb)
   ISBN-13: 978-0-7787-3589-2 (pb)
   ISBN-10: 0-7787-3589-3 (pb)
   1. Golf for children--Juvenile literature. I. Title. II. Series.

   GV966.3.P37 2007
   796.352083--dc22
                                    2007043675

Crabtree Publishing Company

www.crabtreebooks.com   1-800-387-7650

Published in Canada
Crabtree Publishing
616 Welland Ave.
St. Catharines, Ontario
L2M 5V6

Published in the United States
Crabtree Publishing
PMB16A
350 Fifth Ave., Suite 3308
New York, NY 10118

Published by CRABTREE PUBLISHING COMPANY
Copyright © **2008**

CONTENTS

INTRODUCTION

Golf is an outdoor game that can be enjoyed by people of all ages. It is the perfect sport for anyone looking for a new challenge. No two golf courses in the world are the same, so each course you play is a different experience than the last. It is a very relaxing game, and a good way to make new friends. Golf has a unique scoring system that allows players of different skill levels to enjoy playing together. Many celebrities love to play golf in their spare time, and many pro athletes stay active in their off-seasons by golfing. So why not find out for yourself why this sport is so much fun?

ARE YOU LEFT OR RIGHT HANDED?

This book is written from the point of view of a right-handed player.
If you are left handed, remember that the illustrations are the opposite of the position that you should use. Change to use your left hand when the instructions say right hand, and vice versa.

THE GOLF COURSE

Golf is a game that is played over a course of 18 holes. Each hole measures a different length— this length helps to determine the par of the hole. Par is the number of shots that a professional would need on an average day to complete the hole. Players use par as a guide to how many shots it should take them to finish a hole based on their ability.

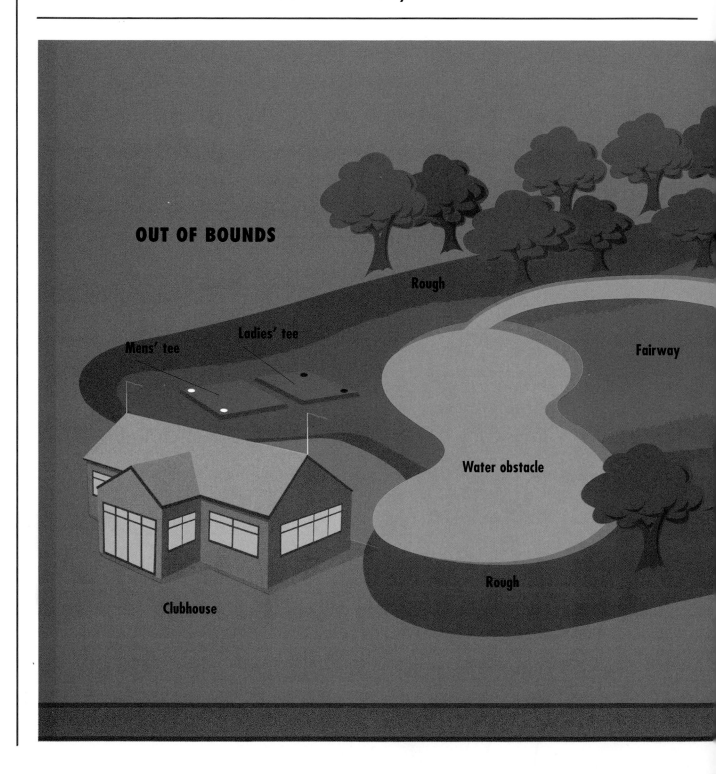

OUT OF BOUNDS

Rough

Ladies' tee

Mens' tee

Fairway

Water obstacle

Rough

Clubhouse

There are three different pars for a golf hole, depending on the length of the hole. They are par 3, par 4, and par 5. Par 3s are the shortest holes, and par 5s are the longest.

The player must hit the ball from the teeing ground toward the green and try to avoid any of the hazards that are on the hole. The hazards can be in the form of water (ponds or streams), sand bunkers, trees, or rough (long grass). Once on the green, the player must get the ball into the hole with the least amount of putts possible.

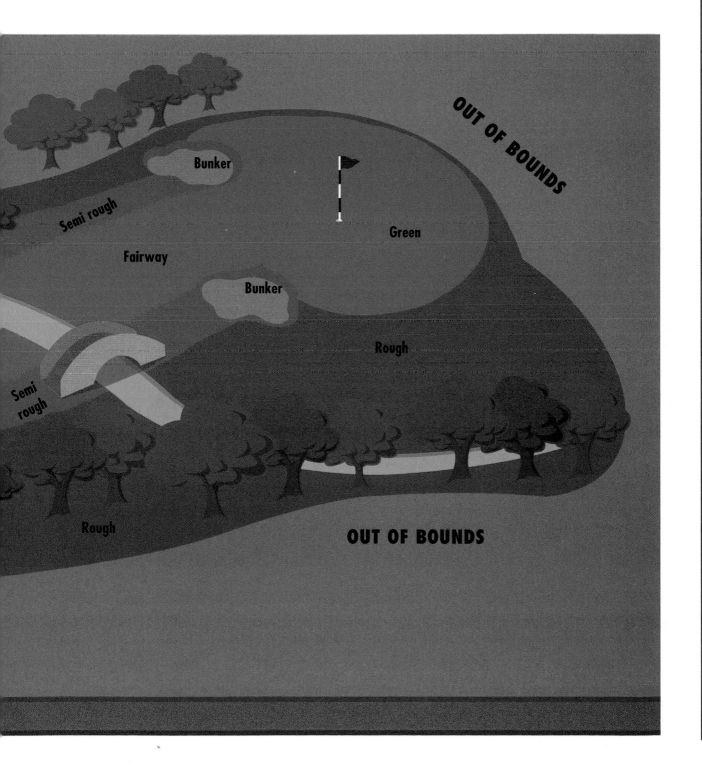

EQUIPMENT—CLUBS

The most important part of a golfer's equipment is their clubs. Each club is designed for a specific type of shot, and will hit the ball to different heights and to different distances. The number of clubs that you need changes from course to course, but you may not have more than 14 clubs in your bag. Clubs are divided into four main categories: irons, wedges, woods, and putters.

IRONS

Irons make up most of a set of clubs. Each club is a different length and has a different amount of loft.
Each club has a number on it. This makes it easier for the player to know how far and how high it will hit the ball.

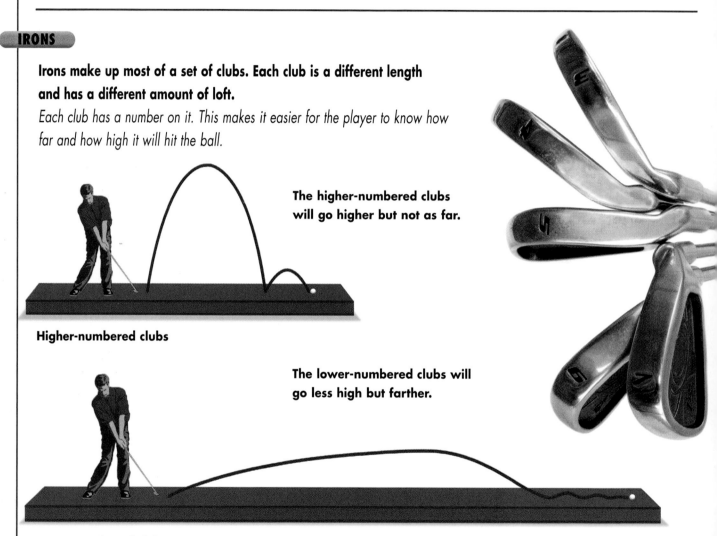

The higher-numbered clubs will go higher but not as far.

Higher-numbered clubs

The lower-numbered clubs will go less high but farther.

Lower-numbered clubs

Irons are the most versatile kind of club. They can be used for many different kinds of shots.
The most common numbered irons are 3, 4, 5, 6, 7, 8, and 9. The 1 to 4 irons are called "long irons", and keep the ball low in the air. The 5 to 7 irons are called "mid irons" and give more lift. The irons that loft the ball the highest are the 8 and 9 irons, which are called "short irons".

TOP TIP
An easy way to remember how each iron works is that the lower the number on the club, the lower the ball will go.

WEDGES

Wedges look like irons, but are designed for a different purpose. The most commonly used wedges have letters instead of numbers on them.

P = PITCHING WEDGE
S = SAND WEDGE

Both of these clubs are designed to hit the ball high into the air so that when it lands on the green, it doesn't roll very far.

The sand wedge is shaped so that it glides through the sand. This makes getting out of the bunkers easier. It can also be used to play shots from the grass.

PUTTERS

Putters are the shortest of all the clubs. They are designed to roll the ball gently along the ground. These clubs are used when the ball is on the green.

Golf clubs are designed for players of average height. Taller or shorter players might need a different length shaft.

WOODS

Woods are the clubs that hit the ball the farthest.

The length and loft angle of these clubs give them great distance. They are called woods because years ago they were actually made from wood!

LOOKING AFTER YOUR CLUBS

Keep your clubs in good condition by cleaning them.

You can soak most club heads in warm water and then clean out the grooves with an old toothbrush. Never submerge a wood in water, though—just wipe it with a damp cloth. Remember to wipe down the golf grips, as well.

OTHER EQUIPMENT

GOLF BALLS

Golf balls come in various colors, but most of them are white.

Balls usually have the manufacturer's name on them and a number. The number helps two players tell their balls apart when they both land close together.

Optic yellow and orange balls are easier to see, especially in frosty or snowy weather.

GOLF BAGS

These can be either carried using the shoulder straps or put onto a cart.

They are used to hold your clubs, spare balls, tees, and all of your other equipment.

TEES

These small pegs can be made of either wood or plastic—plastic is more popular.

Tees are used at the start of each hole on the teeing ground. They hold the ball off of the grass and make it easier to hit. They can only be used on the teeing ground.

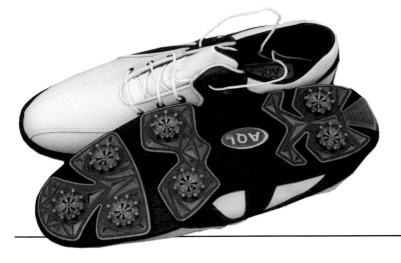

GOLF SHOES

Golf shoes are designed to be comfortable and grip the grass.

Plastic cleats on the soles of the shoes provide extra traction to reduce the chance of slipping as you swing the club. These cleats, or spikes, also provide more grip when walking on steep or wet slopes.

GLOVE

A glove may be worn to provide extra grip on the handle of the club.

Gloves are usually made of leather and are worn on the non-dominant hand. In other words, you would wear them on your left hand if you are right handed, and on your right hand if you are left handed.

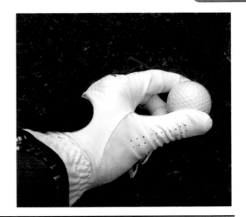

CLOTHING

Golf is a traditional game, and golfers are expected to dress in a certain way.

Shirts should have a collar, and trousers or tailored shorts should be worn. Denim jeans and t-shirts without collars are not considered proper clothing for playing golf. When choosing what to wear, also remember that you need to be comfortable and able to move freely.

An 18-hole golf course can be several miles long. Make sure that your shoes fit well and are comfortable.

WARMING UP

Flexibility is needed for good golfing technique. It can also help you create extra power when you swing the club. Stretching is the best way to improve your flexibility. Perform these simple warm-up exercises to help avoid straining any muscles when you play.

FULL BODY STRETCH

STEP 1

Start by crouching down low with your feet flat on the floor and your hands in front of you.

STEP 2

Stand up, swinging your arms forward and up, until you are standing on your tiptoes with your arms fully stretched toward the sky.

STEP 3

You should inhale as you stretch up. Hold your breath for a moment, and then exhale as you bring your arms down. Return to a normal standing position.

SHOULDER STRETCH

STEP 1

Hold your right arm out in front of you. Pull it across the front of your body. Use the inside of your left elbow to hold the arm in place.

STEP 2

Hold the stretch for 10 seconds. Be careful not to stretch too far— you don't want to hurt yourself.

STEP 3

Repeat the stretch with your left arm.

SIDE STRETCH

LEG STRETCH

Stand back from a wall and place your hands flat against it.
Keep your right leg straight, and bend your left leg at the knee. You should feel the muscles at the back of the right leg being stretched.

Repeat on the other leg.

STEP 1

Place a golf club across the front of your shoulders, keeping it parallel to the ground.

STEP 2

Slowly begin to rotate your shoulders to the right, while keeping your hips pointing forward. When you begin to feel a slight tightness in the side of your body, return to the starting position.

Repeat the stretch by turning in the opposite direction.

The club should remain parallel with the ground during this stretch.

The most common golf injuries come from not warming up properly. These include back pain, shoulder pain, and golfer's elbow—a pain on the inside of the upper arm near the elbow.

WHAT MAKES THE BALL FLY?

Before you learn how to swing the club, it is important that you understand how to strike the ball to get it to fly.

LIFT AND LOFT

The club face strikes the ball below its equator.

The sole of club hits the grass and the ball at the same time.

The club face comes through, creating a divot.

The club face strikes the ball too high (e.g., above its equator).

The ball skids along the ground and never lifts off.

This is often called hitting the ball "too thin".

The club face strikes the ground before striking the ball.

A divot is lifted up, but the ball never flies.

This is often called hitting the ball "too fat".

THE SWEET SPOT

The ideal point on the clubface to make contact with the ball is known as the "sweet spot". This area is located in the center of the clubface. Shots hit from the sweet spot travel faster and farther than shots hit away from center.

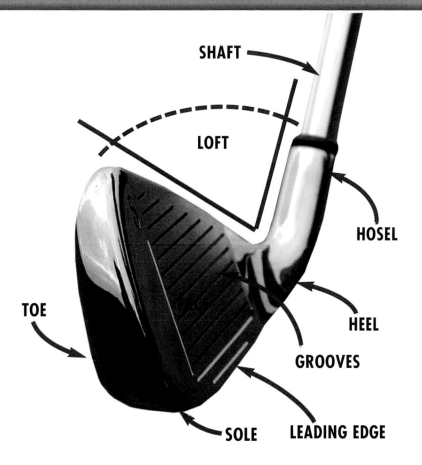

SHAFT

LOFT

HOSEL

TOE

HEEL

GROOVES

SOLE **LEADING EDGE**

SHAFTS

Shafts can be made of steel or graphite.
Graphite shafts can give the ball more distance, but steel shafts are usually more accurate.

Some shafts bend more easily than others—this is called "flex".
Flexible shafts are best for players with slow club speeds. Stiffer shafts are generally used by players with very fast club speeds.

CLUBHEADS

Different kinds of clubhead give different amounts of loft.
The grooves on the clubhead make the ball spin in the air—this is called backspin. This helps carry the ball higher into the air.

The speed at which the clubhead is moving as it hits the ball has a big effect on how far the ball travels.

The average golfer will hit the ball at 80–90 mph (129–145 km/h). Tiger Woods can manage 127 mph (204 km/h)! But the fastest hitter in the world is Sean "The Beast" Fister, who can swing his club at more than 150 mph (241 km/h). Sean was also the World Long Drive Champion in 1995, 2001, and 2005.

Faster speeds = greater distance.
The faster a ball is hit, the farther it will travel.

Slower speed = less distance.
A ball that is hit more gently will travel less far.

AIMING THE CLUB

The way you aim the clubface has a huge effect on the direction in which the ball travels. If you do not aim the face correctly, you will not be able to hit your target.

BALL TO TARGET LINE

To aim the club you must:

STEP 1

First, identify a clear target— for example, the flag.

STEP 2

Imagine a straight line that starts at your ball and goes directly toward your target. This is known as the "ball-to-target line".

HANDY TIPS

TIP 1

Remember that the ball will go in the exact direction that the clubface is pointing. Make sure that you aim the club directly at your target.

TIP 2

Once you have found your ball-to-target line, look for a target on that line that is close to you—such as a fallen leaf.

This object will make it easier to line up an accurate shot.

SQUARE SHOTS

Position the leading edge of the club at a right angle to the ball to target line. This is known as having the clubface 'square' to the ball-to-target line.

OPEN SHOTS

If you aim the club to the left of the ball-to-target line, this is referred to as 'closed', and this will cause the ball to travel to the left of your target.

CLOSED SHOTS

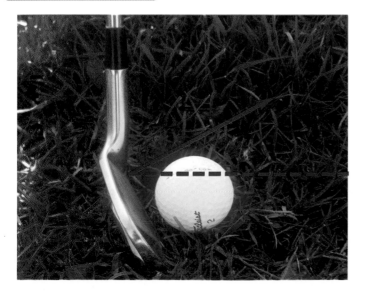

If you aim the club to the right of the ball-to-target line, it is referred to as 'open', and this will cause the ball to travel to the right of your target.

HOLDING THE CLUB CORRECTLY

In the last chapter, you learned how important the clubface is to controling the direction of the ball. In this chapter, you'll learn how to hold the club properly. A correct grip helps you position the clubface for a good swing.

GRIP

The correct position for the club is to have the handle running on a slight diagonal, starting at the middle of the index finger on your left hand and passing just below the base of the little finger.

STEP 1

As you close your left hand on the club, your thumb should be slightly right of center on the handle.

When you look down, you should be able to see two of the knuckles of your left hand.

STEP 2

The top of the handle should extend just over the top of your left hand.

A "V" shape will be created by your index finger and thumb. This "V" should point between your chin and your right shoulder.

STEP 3

The right hand fits into place just below the left hand. The right palm covers the left thumb. The club should fit comfortably into the first three fingers of the right hand. The thumb and index finger of your right hand also create a "V" shape which runs parallel to the "V" on the left hand.

TOP TIP
How tightly you grip the club changes how well the club can be swung. On a scale of one to ten—one being very loose, and ten being very tight—your pressure should be four.

STRONG HOLD

If you hold the club with the V pointing too much to your right, this grip is known as "too strong".

Holding the club in this way could cause the club to point left of the target at impact.

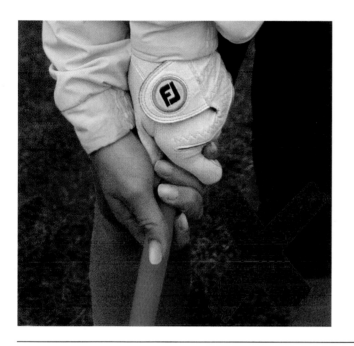

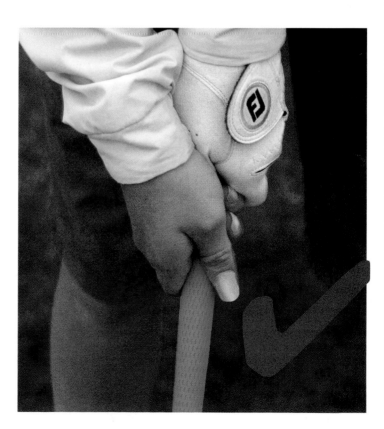

If the V's point is to the left of your chin, it is "too weak".
Holding the club in this way could cause the club to point right of the target at impact.

NEUTRAL HOLD

When you hold the club correctly (as pictured here) it is known as a "neutral hold". This grip is the best way of controling the clubface.

When you begin to play golf, it is tempting to hold the club too tightly. STAY RELAXED. Remember that your holding pressure should be four.

POSTURE—GETTING IT RIGHT

G ood posture is a very important part of learning to play golf. Your posture influences how the club travels around your body, the way the club makes contact with the ground, and your balance during the swing.

ROUTINE FOR CORRECT POSTURE

If you want to make successful golf swings, you must first learn how to stand correctly. The best way to achieve correct posture is by following the routine below:

STEP 1

Holding the club properly, stand with your legs straight and your feet shoulder width apart.

STEP 2

Hold your arms out straight in front of you so that the club shaft is parallel to the ground and waist high.

Your body weight should be evenly distributed on both feet.

TOP TIP

Golf courses are not always flat, so adjust your posture according to the slope. If you are facing uphill, more of your weight should be on your right leg. When facing downhill, more of your weight should be on your left leg.

STEP 3

Tilt your upper body forward from the hips so that the club moves toward the ground. As you lean forward, you may feel the muscles in the backs of your legs tighten—this feeling is normal.

Feet are shoulder width apart

STEP 4

Bend your knees slightly—this will take away any tightness in your legs and make you more stable.

SIMPLE CHECKPOINTS

*1) Your arms should feel as though they are hanging from your shoulders.
There will be a space between your hands and your legs.
2) Your chin should be lifted up and away from your chest.
This creates room for your shoulders to turn.
3) Watching another player in this position from the front, his or her right shoulder
should be slightly lower than the left shoulder. This is because the right hand
is lower than the left hand on the handle of the club.*

BODY ALIGNMENT

You have already learned how to improve your aim by imagining a line from your ball to the target—the ball-to-target line. This line also plays in an important part in helping position your body correctly.

PARALLEL RAILWAY TRACKS

As you will remember, the clubface must point directly at the target—in other words, it should be square to the ball-to-target line. You must now get your body parallel to this line. It may help to imagine that you are standing on a railway track.

STEP 1
Think of the right side of the track as the ball-to-target line, which heads straight to your target. Your clubface should be aimed in this direction.

STEP 2
The left side of the track is where your feet are positioned. This imaginary line should be parallel to the right-hand side of the track.

STEP 3

The easiest way to do this is by starting with your feet together and then carefully moving them apart one at a time.

Notice that the right shoulder is lower than the left. This is because right-handed players have their right hand placed below their left. This will be reversed for a left-handed player.

STEP 4

You must also get your knees, hips and shoulders all pointing in the same direction as your feet.

Once you are parallel to the "train tracks", your body will be aligned correctly for your shot.

FULL SWING WITH A WOOD

Wood shots are played when a long distance needs to be covered. Woods are the power clubs—the most powerful of these clubs is the number 1 wood. The number 1 wood is commonly called the "driver". The driver is generally used at the start of each hole on the teeing ground. A tee is used to lift the ball off the ground when you are using the driver.

TEEING-UP THE BALL

When using the driver, the ball must be put onto a tee.

STEP 1

It is important that the height of the tee is correct. A simple way to place the ball at the correct height is to line up the equator of the ball with the top of the driver.

equator of golf ball

STEP 2

This position lifts the ball off the ground enough to allow the club to sweep the ball off the tee without the bottom of the club hitting the ground.

THE SET UP

STEP 1

Position your feet slightly wider than your shoulders— this will provide better balance with the longer wood club. Place your left heel in line with the tee. This position will help create a sweeping action with the club.

THE TAKE AWAY

THE BACKSWING

Hands are at
hip height

Shoulders turn while
left forearm is at right
angle to shaft of club

Weight shifts onto
right foot

STEP 2
Turn your shoulders back to start the take away.

*As your hands reach hip height, the shaft of the club
should be parallel with your feet and the ball-to-target line.*

STEP 3
*Your shoulders continue to turn, and your body weight moves
toward the inside of the right foot.*

THE BACKSWING: PART TWO

Left shoulder is underneath the chin

Left arm remains straight

Upper body starts to turn

Legs barely move

STEP 4

Bend your wrists, keeping the right angle between your left forearm and the shaft of the club.

As your upper body turns, your legs should stay straight and only move slightly. This lower body resistance helps create a lot of the power in the golf swing.

Your left arm should remain straight, and your shoulders should be fully turned. Your left shoulder is now underneath your chin.

THE DOWNSWING

STEP 5

The downswing begins with your hips moving toward the target, as they begin to unwind.

Move your body weight onto your left foot, and move your shoulders and arms forward toward your target.

TOP TIP
When you are taking your club back, your eyes should remain on the ball, and your head should hardly move.

IMPACT

THE FOLLOW-THROUGH

Head behind ball

Right heel starts to lift off ground

Weight on left side

STEP 6

As the club hits the ball, your hips should have turned beyond their original starting position (the set up—page 22).

Your weight should be mostly on your left side, and your right heel begins to lift off the ground. Your head should still be behind the ball at this point. The clubhead sweeps the ball off of the tee without touching the ground.

STEP 7

After the impact, continue to turn your hips and shoulders toward the target.

Move your weight onto your left foot, and raise your right foot so that it's on its toes. Your knees should finish close together. You will be balancing on your left foot, with the club behind your head.

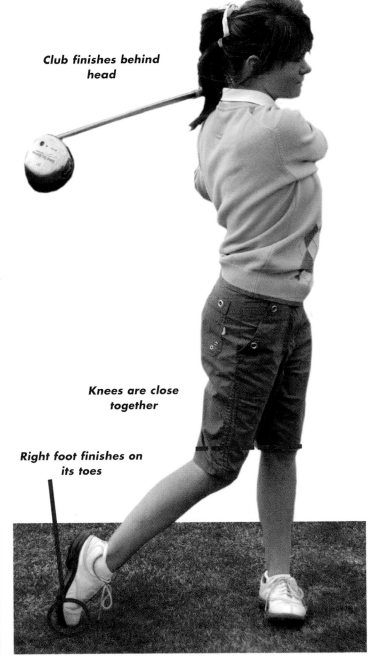

Club finishes behind head

Knees are close together

Right foot finishes on its toes

FULL SWING WITH AN IRON (7 IRON)

*I*rons are used for shorter shots than woods—they are taken from the fairway as you are approaching the green. The number of the club that you use depends on how far it is to the green. Lower-numbered irons are used from longer distances, and higher-numbered irons are used from closer range.

THE SET UP

Front view

Side view

STEP 1

Make sure that the club is aimed correctly at the target. Check that you have proper body posture and alignment.

You can see from the photo on the right that the ball should be positioned in the middle of your feet. This position helps you strike the ball and the ground correctly. It also helps produce the correct amount of spin.

THE TAKE AWAY

The take away starts when you turn your shoulders.

STEP 2

As your hands reach hip height, the shaft of the club should be parallel with both your feet and the ball-to-target line.

STEP 3

As you move your hands above waist height, start to bend your wrists. By the time the left arm is in a horizontal position, your wrists should be fully bent.

Weight transfers to right foot

STEP 4

Continue to turn your shoulders, as you move your body weight toward the inside of your right foot.

As your upper body turns, your legs should hold their positions and move only slightly. This lower-body resistance creates most of the power in the golf swing.

Keep your left arm straight, as you fully turn your shoulders. Your left shoulder should now be underneath your chin.

Arms and shoulders move in direction of target

STEP 5

The downswing begins with the hips moving toward the target (the flag) as they begin to unwind.

Move your body weight onto your left foot, as you bring your shoulders and arms forward toward the target.

Weight moves back to left foot

IMPACT

Compare the straight posture from Step 1 (above) to the turned body position in Step 6 (right).

Hips turned
toward target

Weight on
left side

Heel starts
to lift

STEP 6

When the club strikes the ball, your hips should have turned beyond their original starting position during the set up.

Your weight should now be largely on your left side, and your right heel has started to lift off of the ground.

The sole (bottom) of the club makes contact with the grass. This enables the loft of the club to lift the ball off of the ground.

THE FOLLOW–THROUGH

STEP 7

Continue to turn your hips and shoulders toward the target. Your weight moves completely onto the left foot. As this happens, lift your right foot up to finish on its toes.

Hips and shoulders move toward target

Club finishes behind head

Knees close together

Right foot finishes on its toes

Your knees finish close together. You finish balancing on your left foot, with the club behind your head.

Balance is a key ingredient to a successful golf shot—swing the club smoothly and evenly to stay stable.

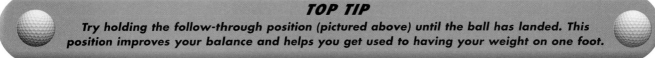

TOP TIP
Try holding the follow-through position (pictured above) until the ball has landed. This position improves your balance and helps you get used to having your weight on one foot.

PITCHING

A pitch shot is usually played from inside 100 yards of the green. This shot can be done with either the pitching or sand wedge. A pitch shot is perfect when you are trying to hit the ball over the top of a hazard, such as a bunker or stream. It is also useful if the ground between your ball and the green is uneven, because you can lift the ball right over the problem.

THE SET UP

A good pitch sends the ball high in the air so that it stops quickly when it lands on the green. It is not a full-power shot—control the length of your swing to get the right shot distance.

STEP 1

Start with your feet slightly closer than shoulder width apart.

Hold the club 1 to 2 inches farther down the handle than normal.

STEP 2

Position the ball in the center of your feet. About 60% of your body weight should be on your left foot and 40% on your right.

THE BACKSWING

STEP 3

Bend your wrists so that the club shaft creates a right angle with the left forearm.

The shorter the backswing length, the less power is generated for the shot.

TEMPO

Smooth

STEP 4

Good pitching requires an even tempo throughout the shot. A jerky or uneven action will make a poor pitch shot.

THE FOLLOW-THROUGH

STEP 5

Finish with your body weight on your left foot and your upper body facing the target. Your right foot is slightly raised.

The length of your follow through should be about the same as the length of your backswing.

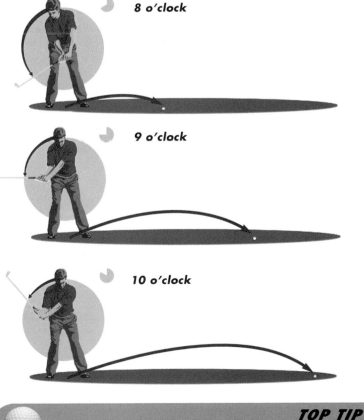

8 o'clock

9 o'clock

10 o'clock

DISTANCE CONTROL

Knowing how far the ball will travel is important to making a successful pitch shot. The power and distance of the shot depends mostly on the length of the backswing.

Imagine that you are in the center of a clock face, and you have a choice of three different backswing positions: 8 o'clock, 9 o'clock, and 10 o'clock. Using your left forearm as the guide, allow your backswing to go to one of these three positions.

You will notice that the farther back your arm goes, the farther your shot travels. With practice and experience you will learn which swing length you need to make a particular shot.

TOP TIP

Remember that the later the clock time you swing to, the farther the ball will go.

CHIPPING

A chip shot is used when the ball is almost on the green. The aim is to get the ball as close to the hole as possible. A good chip shot gently lifts the ball onto the putting green and toward the hole. Power is not a big part of chipping—it is more important to have a light, even touch to your shot. Any golfer can master the chip once they understand some of the keys to its technique.

THE SET UP

Various clubs can be used to play a chip shot—each club produces different amounts of flight and roll.

STEP 1

Hold the club lower down so that your right hand is near the bottom of the handle—this grip will give you extra control.

Keep your feet close together. 60% of your weight should be on your left side, and 40% on your right.

THE STROKE

The ball should be positioned in line with the inside of your right foot.

STEP 2

Unlike full shots and pitch shots, you do not bend your wrists when chipping. Use a small backswing, and keep the clubhead below your waist.

This movement is a pendulum-style action that comes from the shoulders, not your elbows. Keep your arms straight.

A key to successful chipping is choosing the correct club. Each club has a different loft, which affects how the ball flies when it is chipped. The diagram below shows you how the ball will react differently when it is struck with different numbered clubs.

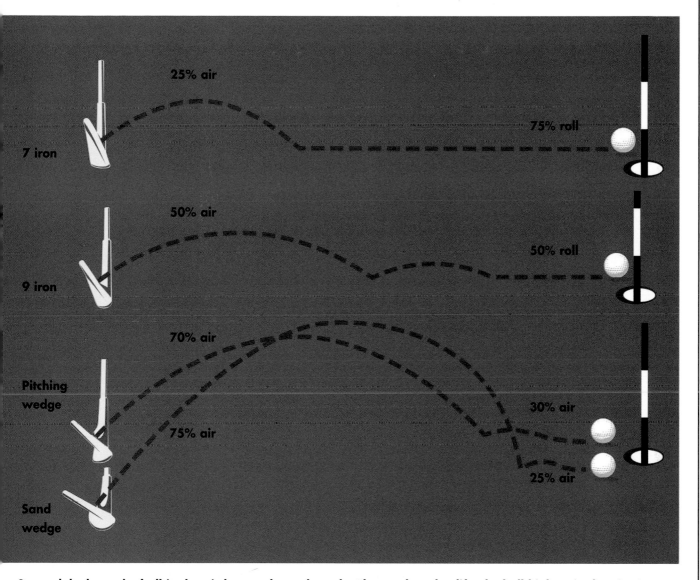

Some clubs keep the ball in the air longer than others do. The sand wedge lifts the ball highest in the air—it needs this extra lift to get the ball out of deep bunkers. Knowing the difference between these clubs is important to getting the ball onto the green and close to the hole.

When you find yourself chipping onto the green, you should ask yourself these two questions:

1 Where exactly do I want the ball to land before it rolls across the green?
2 Where is this chosen spot found in between the ball and the hole?
(Is it, for example, 50% of the way to the hole?)

Once you have answered these questions, you can use the information from this diagram to choose the best club for the job. For example, if the landing point is halfway to the hole, then you need the 9 iron (50% air/50% roll).

BUNKER SHOTS

Bunkers are placed around the golf course as a type of hazard. They are pits in the ground filled with sand, and you need a specific technique to play them correctly. The most common bunkers are greenside bunkers. These hazards are found in front or to the side of the green. They catch any shot played toward the green that is slightly off line. The club used to play from a greenside bunker is the sand wedge.

SPLASH SHOTS

A bunker shot is also called a "splash shot" because sand splashes into the air as the shot is hit. When this shot is played correctly, the club never touches the ball. The club hits the sand, and the momentum of the sand lifts the ball up and out.

THE SET UP

STEP 1

For this shot, you want to cut slightly across the ball—your body alignment is pointing to the left.

The clubface is facing upward but still points toward the flagstick. Your grip should only have one knuckle showing—this makes sure that the clubface doesn't close (turn left) as it strikes the sand.

The ball position should be about two inches to the left of center of the feet.

WHERE YOUR FEET SHOULD BE

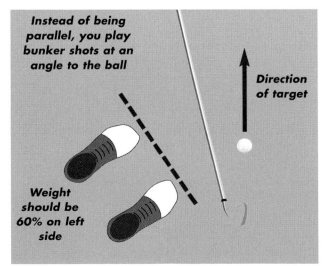

Instead of being parallel, you play bunker shots at an angle to the ball

Direction of target

Weight should be 60% on left side

THE TAKEAWAY

STEP 2

As the shoulders begin to turn, your wrists bend almost immediately, making the club parallel to the ground.

THE BACKSWING

STEP 3

The length of your backswing depends on how far the ball needs to travel.

The farther the ball needs to go, the longer your backswing.

THE DOWNSWING

STEP 4

As the club moves down toward the ball, your eyes should be focused on the sand about two inches behind the ball.

The club should strike the sand about two inches behind the ball. Your club will gather sand and lift the ball up out of the bunker.

The position of the ball in your stance allows the ball to be lifted from the bunker with the momentum of the sand.

THE FOLLOW-THROUGH

STEP 5

After playing the shot, your upper body should face the target. Most of your body weight finishes on the left side. Your arms follow through to about the same distance as your backswing.

TOP TIP

When you play a bunker shot, the clubhead is not allowed to touch the sand before your shot. Remember to hover the club above the sand before playing the shot.

PUTTING

The putter is used when the player's ball is on the green. The player uses the putter to roll the ball along the green and into the hole—the ball does not lift into the air as it does in other shots. The player needs get the ball into the hole with as few putts as possible—each try counts as a shot.

THE GRIP

The putter's handle is shaped differently than on the other clubs.

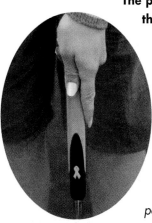

Most clubs have round handles, but putter handles have a flat front. This is a good reminder that the putter should be held differently.

STEP 1

Place the left hand on the handle so that the thumb is on the flat part and pointing straight down toward the ground.

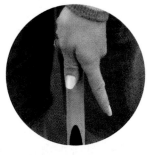

STEP 2

Lift the index finger off of the handle to make room for your right hand.

STEP 3

Grip the club with the right hand. Make sure that all four fingers of the right hand are placed underneath your raised left index finger.

STEP 4

Place your right thumb onto the flat part of the handle so that it points toward the ground.

THE SET UP

STEP 1

Your feet should be shoulder width apart with the ball slightly to the left of center.

Your body tilts forward from the hips. Your hands hang down and under your shoulders.

STEP 2

Your knees should be slightly flexed, and your eyes should be directly over the ball.

line of sight

The putter moves in a pendulum-style motion that is created by gently rocking the shoulders.

STEP 1

The wrists should not bend during the putting stroke—keep them straight.

Keep an even tempo throughout the stroke—this helps you develop a better feel for the speed of the greens.

STEP 2

Try to make the lengths of your backswing and follow-through the same.

Putting greens are not flat. It is important to check which way the green is sloping, so you can decide where to aim their ball. Working this out is known as "reading the green"—good golfers are able to judge these slopes and angles very well.

To read the green, crouch down behind the ball, and get low to the ground. From here, you can see the slope of the green more clearly—from the higher standing position, everything looks flat.

The slope will make the ball curve as it rolls along the green—this curve is known as "break". You must try to estimate the amount of break that you think there will be on a putt. Then you aim your putter to make up for the curve. For example, if you think that the ball will curve 12 inches from left to right, aim the putter 12 inches to the left of the hole. That way, the ball will (hopefully) curl into the hole.

Practice aiming at a small target.
Try aiming at a tee placed into the green. This smaller target will help you improve your aiming skills. Afterward, a golf hole looks like a really big target in comparison. This exercise will also improve your confidence on the greens.

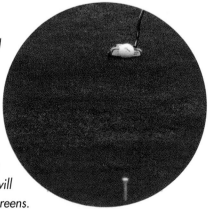

TOP TIP
Try not to leave putts short of the hole. If you always hit the ball hard enough for it to reach the hole, you can quickly become a successful putter.

SAFETY

Safety is an important part of golf. A speeding ball shot through the air or a quickly swung club can be very dangerous. It is important to be aware of these potential dangers. Remember to watch out for other golfers on the course, and not just your own playing partners.

SHOUTING "FORE"

When a golf ball is flying through the air, it can be traveling very fast. For example, a professional golfer hitting a ball with a driver hits the ball at a speed of around 160 mph (257 km/h)!

If your shot accidentally travels toward other players, you must warn them that they could be in danger so that they can protect themselves. You do this by shouting the word "fore" as loudly as possible. The word "fore" is believed to have started in the military. It was a warning for troops to take cover when something was fired behind them.

HEARING "FORE"

If you are playing golf and you hear someone else shout "fore" you should:

A) *Put your arms up around your head for protection.*

B) *Make yourself as small a target as possible by crouching down. **NEVER** turn to see who shouted fore—a ball could be headed straight for you!*

STANDING IN THE SAFE ZONE

Never stand too close to other golfers when they're taking shots.

*Remember that a golfer needs plenty of space when swinging a club. The safe zone is behind, facing, and slightly to the right of the player. **NEVER** stand directly behind him or her, or you may get hit by the club as he or she swings.*

DIET

A balanced diet will help you both on and off the golf course. A healthy diet consists of a combination of carbohydrates, proteins and fats—together they will provide you with the nutrients that your body needs.

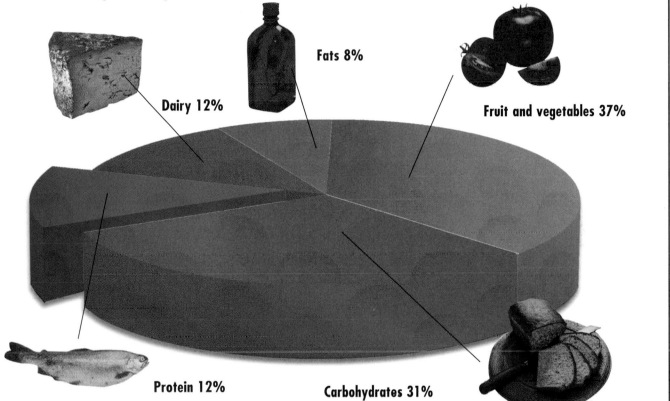

Dairy 12%

Fats 8%

Fruit and vegetables 37%

Protein 12%

Carbohydrates 31%

Golf is a game that can take over four hours to play, and it is important that you keep your energy level up during the round.

Carry fruit, cereal bars, and plenty of water in your bag to snack on during your round. Avoid eating a large meal just before play. A healthy meal eaten two to three hours before the start of the game is best. Drink plenty of water during the day and throughout your round. This will keep you hydrated and help make sure that your body can perform to the best of its ability.

Flexibility is key to being a top golfer. Use the stretching exercises on pages 10-11 to help improve your flexibility.

Golf involves a lot of walking, often over steep hills. When a golfer becomes tired, it becomes harder to concentrate and easier to make mistakes. If you are fit, you can have an advantage over your opponents—you'll always feel fresh and alert on the course.

MENTAL SKILLS

This section is designed to help you develop the mental skills needed to play golf. A round of golf can take over four hours, so it is important that you learn how and when to concentrate.

CONCENTRATION

First, you should understand that you don't need to concentrate for every minute that you are on the course. In fact, to concentrate for such a long time is almost impossible!

You only really need to concentrate when you are about to play a shot—you'll need about one minute of concentration per shot. If you play 80 shots in a four-hour round, then you need to concentrate for about a quarter of the time, or one hour.

If you tried to concentrate continuously from the first tee to the 18th green, you would be mentally exhausted long before you finished the round!

CONCENTRATING WHEN IT MATTERS

Learn to use your concentration only when you need it—think of your concentration like an hourglass with the sand inside.

All golfers start with the same amount of concentration, but it is then up to them how they use it.

Players who don't relax between shots find that all of the sand runs out of their hourglass long before the end of their rounds.

Good players understand that by relaxing between shots, they are saving valuable concentration. This allows them to play all 18 holes without their concentration running out.

By thinking about other things between shots, you will make it easier for you to blot out distracting thoughts when you're taking a shot.

TOP TIP

One way to relax is to look at wildlife. By counting the different types of animals you see, you can help your brain recharge so that it is ready for the next shot.

When you hit a bad shot, it can be disappointing, but don't get upset.

If you give in to stress and negative feelings, you will play worse. When you expect to mess up a shot, the chances are that you will. Try to keep a positive mental attitude—this will help you concentrate and play confidently. 90% of winning is in the mind!

To play good golf, you must learn how to control your temper. When you hit a bad shot or have some bad luck, getting angry and losing your temper makes you lose your concentration.

All golfers hit poor shots from time to time—even the pros! A good golfer quickly forgets about the bad shot and gets ready for the next shot.

BODY LANGUAGE

A golfer that is sulking is easy to spot on the course because his or her body language is poor.

He or she tend to walk slowly and without purpose. His or her head is always looking down at the ground.

Good players walk with a spring in their step. They have their heads up and looking straight ahead. They are aware of their surroundings and move with a purpose.

Try to walk with this type of body language between your shots. It will help you be positive when it's time for your next shot.

Remember: champions hit bad shots, too, but they put their mistakes behind them and move on.

HOW THE PROS DO IT

Most people play golf to relax and have fun, but a few lucky, talented players are professional golfers. These players travel the world and can be paid huge sums of money if they are successful.

Tiger Woods was born in Cypress, California, on December 30, 1975. He later studied at Stanford University and became a key member of the college golf team. Since he turned pro in 1996, he's taken the golfing world by storm.

He won his first major, the 1997 Masters, at the age of 21, making him the youngest player in history to win the event. He won by 12 shots with a winning score of 18 under-par—an all time scoring record for the Augusta course.

To date, he has won 13 major championships and is on target to beat the record of 18 majors, which is held by Jack Nicklaus.

So far he has won prize money of over $74,000,000. When you add to that the money he receives from his sponsors and advertising, he is one of the richest athletes in the world.

Born October 11 1989, Michelle Wie started playing golf at the age of four in Hawaii. By the time she was eleven, she was regularly winning competitions, often beating her male counterparts.

Growing up, she followed the career of Tiger Woods, and this convinced her that she also wanted to be a professional golfer.

At 6 feet (180 cm) tall Michelle can drive the ball over 280 yards (256 m), and her talent at such a young age has helped her become only the fourth female in history to play in a PGA Tour event.

Playing in the Sony Open in January 2004, Michelle missed the halfway cut by only one shot and scored better than 47 men along the way. At the same time, she became the youngest player ever to play in a PGA Tour event—she was 14.

In October 2007, Michelle turned 18 and was allowed to join the LPGA (Ladies' Professional Golf Association).

WHERE THE PROS PLAY

ST. ANDREWS, SCOTLAND

Golf has been played at St. Andrews, in Scotland, since around 1400. The old course is known throughout the world as the "Home of Golf".

What was a simple track hacked through the bushes has become six links golf courses and four other courses in the immediate area, including the Duke's Course. These courses attract hundreds of thousands of golfing fans from around the world every year.

AUGUSTA NATIONAL, USA

Augusta National, in Georgia, is home to the first major golf tournament each year—The Masters. It is arguably the most beautiful golf setting in the world.

This picture-perfect setting includes the famous Amen Corner, which consists of three holes (the 11th, 12th and 13th). These holes may be beautiful, but they are also some of the most difficult on the course.

PEBBLE BEACH, USA

Pebble Beach is located on the famous 17-Mile Drive in California. This area is one of the most stunning coastlines to be found anywhere in the world.

It has been used to host the U.S. Open on several occasions, the most famous one being in 2000, when Tiger Woods won the event by a record-breaking 15 shots.

Jack Nicklaus was once quoted as saying "If I only had one more round to play, I would choose to play it at Pebble Beach. I loved this course from the first time I saw it. It's possibly the best in the world."

GOLF RULES

There are many rules in golf that cover all types of situations. On these pages, you will find some of the basic rules that will help you as you learn to play golf.

TAKING A DROP

There are some instances during the game where you can pick up the ball and move it—sometimes with a penalty shot and sometimes for free.

To drop the ball, you must stand upright, hold the ball at shoulder height and arm's length, and simply let it go. If it accidentally touches you, your partner, or equipment and rolls closer to the hole, you must drop the ball again.

A penalty shot is one that is added to your score for errors such as hitting the ball into a water hazard.

LOOKING FOR THE BALL

If you hit your ball but are unsure of where it landed (e.g., in long grass) you are allowed five minutes to look for it.

If you have not found it after five minutes, the ball is considered lost. You must go back to where you played your previous shot and drop another ball into play under a penalty.

GROUNDING THE CLUB

Grounding the club is when the sole of the club touches the ground before you play a stroke. In a bunker or water hazard, you are not allowed to ground your club before you hit the ball.

CLEANING THE BALL

When a ball is on the putting green, it may be necessary to pick it up and clean it. This will remove mud, grit, or moisture from the ball.

Cleaning helps make sure that the ball rolls smoothly across the green. Before it can be moved, its position must be marked.

> **Some courses have ballwashers by the tees. These should be used before teeing off to ensure that the ball rolls smoothly.**

PLAYING THE BALL AS IT LIES

You are generally not allowed to bend or break anything growing or fixed (e.g., snapping a branch) to improve the position of your ball—except while playing a shot.

You are allowed to remove obstacles such as stones, fallen leaves, or twigs without penalty, except when you're in a hazard.

PROVISIONAL BALL

If you think tht your ball could be out of bounds or lost, you may play a provisional ball.

You must say that it is a provisional ball before it is played. If the original ball is lost, you continue with the provisional ball under penalty of one stroke. If the old ball is found, you play with it and stop using the provisional ball.

PENALTY FOR A LOST BALL

If a player's ball is lost or hit out of bounds, he or she must play another ball under penalty of one shot. The new ball is dropped as near as possible to the spot where the original ball was last played.

CASUAL WATER AND ABNORMAL GROUND CONDITIONS

If your ball is in casual water (such as a puddle), ground under repair, or a hole made by a burrowing animal (such as a rabbit), you may drop the ball anywhere within one club length of the obstruction without penalty. You must drop on the side farthest away from the hole—you cannot move your ball closer to the hole.

HOW TO KEEP SCORE & ETIQUETTE

The number of times that the ball is hit is counted from the first shot on each hole to the final shot when the ball goes in the hole.

SCORECARD

This score is recorded on a scorecard. When all 18 holes are completed, the total score is added together.
If you attempt to hit the ball and miss, it still counts as a shot. This is called an "air shot," and must be added to your score.

GOLF HANDICAP

A player's standard can be determined by his or her handicap. This is a number that tells us on average how many shots over the total par of the course the player tends to score.

If the total par for a course is 72 and on average the player takes 82 shots, then the handicap is 10. This system allows players of different skill levels to play against each other. By subtracting their handicaps from their scores, you can work out the winner. The maximum handicap is 28 for men and 36 for women.

INFORMATION ON A SCORE CARD

Name of the competition

Men's competition holes

Men's regular holes

Par for the hole

Your handicap

Men's stroke index (difficulty of holes)

The SSS (Standard Scratch Score) measures a course's difficulty. It is used for competition purposes, and to calculate your handicap.

Date and time

Your name

Hole number

The score of the person marking the card

Distances to the hole. There are different distances, and they are all color coded.

Your scores

Your total score for the first nine holes

Ladies stroke index (Difficulty of holes)

COMPETITION										S.S.S		
DATE		TIME		H'CAP	Strokes Rec'd	ENTRY NO:			H'CAP	Strokes Rec'd	WHITE	71
PLAYER A:							B:				YELLOW	69
PLAYER C:							D:				RED	72

HOLE	MARKERS SCORE	WHITE YARDS	PAR	YELLOW YARDS	STROKE INDEX	SCORE A	B	C	D	Net SCORE	POINTS W=+, L=- H=0	RED YARDS	PAR	STROKE INDEX
1		547	5	524	11							453	5	9
2		349	4	326	9							263	4	17
3		430	4	399	1							359	4	5
4		177	3	164	17							175	3	15
5		378	4	346	5							320	4	11
6		555	5	518	13							442	5	1
7		345	4	325	15							292	4	13
8		186	3	173	7							159	3	7
9		440	4	409	3							357	4	3
Out		3407	36	3184								2873	36	

Please avoid slow play at all times!

10		357	4	333	14							297	4	16
11		527	5	495	8							435	5	4
12		177	3	161	6							136	3	6
13		501	5	475	4							423	5	2
14		173	3	155	18							152	3	18
15		340	4	309	16							279	4	10
16		376	4	350	12							327	4	14
17		207	3	184	2							156	3	8
18		509	5	482	10							436	5	12
In		3167	36	2944								2631	36	
Out		3407	36	3184								2873	36	
Total		6574	72	6128								5454	72	
					Handicap									
					Net									

Your total score for the first nine holes

Your total score for the second nine holes

Your overall score

The signature of the person marking the card

Marker's Signature

Player's Signature

Your handicap

Your overall score minus your handicap

Your signature

GOLF IS A QUIET GAME

Never shout, talk loudly, or call out to friends. If you are too noisy, you can distract other golfers and spoil their fun.

HELP FELLOW GOLFERS

If they are searching for their balls, help them look. You may want their help looking for a ball later.

ALWAYS SHAKE HANDS

Congratulate your fellow players at the end of the round. This is a sign of good sportsmanship, which is a key part of golf.

PLAY WITHOUT DELAY

Move off of the green as soon as the last player holes out, and record the scores on the next tee. This can save a great deal of time over the round.

WATCH YOUR BALL

Keep your eye on the ball until it has stopped. If you lose sight of your ball, it can add time to your round in extra searching for the ball.

LET FASTER PLAYERS PLAY THROUGH

If a group is playing faster behind you, let them through. To do this, just move to a safe area at the side of the hole, and wave the group behind you through.

BEHAVE IN A COURTEOUS MANNER

Club throwing, bad language, and cheating are not allowed in golf.

GLOSSARY

AIM – The direction in which the clubface points, affecting the flight direction of the ball.

BODY ALIGNMENT – The direction in which a player's body faces as he or she prepare to play a shot.

BREAK – The curve on the ball caused by slopes on the putting green.

BUNKER – A hole in ground filled with sand, designed as an obstacle.

CASUAL WATER – A temporary collection of water on a course that is not part of a water hazard (e.g., a puddle).

CLUBFACE – The part of the golf club that is used to make contact with the ball.

FAIRWAY – The area of short-cut grass that is best for playing shots from.

FLAGSTICK – This is used to indicate the location of the hole on the putting green.

FORE – A warning used to inform fellow golfers that they may be in danger of being struck by a ball.

GREEN – A smooth, prepared grass area where the flag and hole are located.

GROUND UNDER REPAIR (GUR) – An area of the course that has been marked out by the maintenance committee crew for repair.

HOLE – The target of the game, into which the ball must be driven. A hole is also a division of the golf course—there are 18 holes on a course.

IMPACT – The moment during the swing when the clubface makes contact with the ball.

IRONS – Irons are individually numbered and make up a majority of any golfer's set of clubs. Each iron will hit the ball a different height and distance.

LOFT – The angle on the golf club that controls the height of a ball and the distance that it flies.

LOOSE IMPEDIMENT – Natural objects that include stones, twigs, and branches. These can be moved, provided that they are not growing, solidly embedded, or stuck to the ball.

PAR – Target score of a professional golfer for each hole.

POSTURE – The position that the body should be in while holding the golf club.

PUTT – A type of shot played using a specific club—the putter—to roll the ball into the hole.

ROUGH – Long grass that makes playing a shot more difficult.

TEE – A device that is designed to raise the ball off of the ground. A tee must be no more than four inches tall.

TEEING GROUND – The starting point for each hole.

TEMPO – The speed and rhythm with which the body and club moves.

WATER HAZARD – Any sea, lake, pond, river, or ditch that is defined by the yellow stakes.

WEDGES – These clubs have the specific purpose of making the ball fly high so that it stops quickly when landing.

WOODS – The longest and most powerful clubs in a set, designed to hit the ball long distances.

INDEX

Printed in the USA